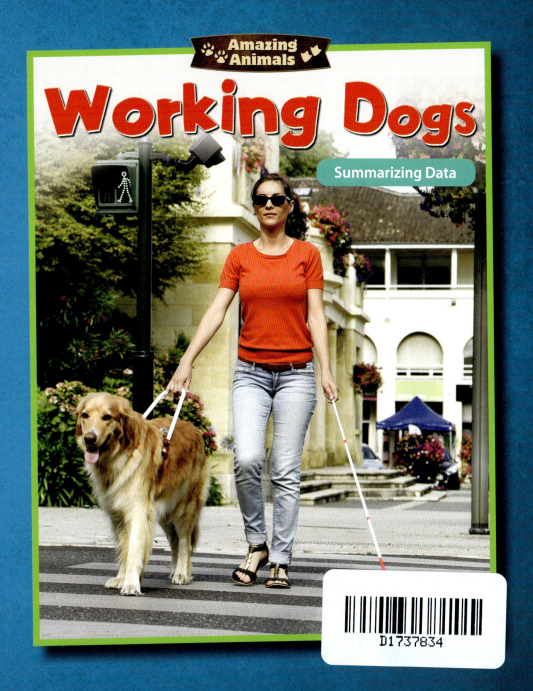

Amazing Animals
Working Dogs
Summarizing Data

Lisa MacDonald

Contributing Author

Alison S. Marzocchi, Ph.D.

Consultant

Colleen Pollitt, M.A.Ed.
Math Support Teacher
Howard County Public Schools

Publishing Credits

Rachelle Cracchiolo, M.S.Ed., *Publisher*
Conni Medina, M.A.Ed., *Editor in Chief*
Dona Herweck Rice, *Series Developer*
Emily R. Smith, M.A.Ed., *Series Developer*
Diana Kenney, M.A.Ed., NBCT, *Content Director*
Stacy Monsman, M.A., *Editor*
Michelle Jovin, M.A., *Associate Editor*
Fabiola Sepulveda, *Graphic Designer*

Image Credits: p.7 (top) Akimov Igor/Shutterstock; p.7 (middle) Steve Skjold/Alamy; p.7 (bottom) Belish/Shutterstock; p.8 (bottom left) Rich T Photo/Shutterstock; p.8 (bottom right) Akimov Igor/Shutterstock; p.9 (bottom) Cylonphoto/iStock; p.11 (top left) Jim Holden/Alamy; p.11 (top right) Lee Busby/Mirrorpix/Newscom; p.11 (bottom) PA Images/Alamy; p.14, p.15 (top) AP Photo/Allen G. Breed; p.15 (bottom) Trong Nguyen/Shutterstock; p.17 (top) Stocktrek Images, Inc./Alamy; p.17 (bottom) deepspace/Shutterstock; p.19 (top) Elf/Wikimedia Commons; p.20 U.S. Air Force, photo by Tech. Sgt. Nieko Carzis; p.21 (both) United States Marine Corps photo by Cpl. Tom Sloan; p.2 (top) Imagine China/Newscom; p.22 (bottom) Bill Greenblatt/UPI/Newscom; p.24 (middle) Oleksii Chumachenko/Shutterstock; p.24 (bottom) Belish/Shutterstock; p.26 (bottom) Leonard Zhukovsky/Shutterstock; all other images from iStock and/or Shutterstock.

Library of Congress Cataloging-in-Publication Data

Names: MacDonald, Lisa, author.
Title: Working dogs : summarizing data / Lisa MacDonald.
Description: Huntington Beach, CA : Teacher Created Materials, [2019] | Series: Amazing animals | Audience: Grade 4 to 6. | Includes index. | Identifiers: LCCN 2018051882 (print) | LCCN 2018052960 (ebook) | ISBN 9781425855390 (eBook) | ISBN 9781425858957 (paperback)
Subjects: LCSH: Working dogs--Juvenile literature.
Classification: LCC SF428.2 (ebook) | LCC SF428.2 .M28 2019 (print) | DDC 636.7/0886--dc23
LC record available at https://lccn.loc.gov/2018051882

Teacher Created Materials

5301 Oceanus Drive
Huntington Beach, CA 92649-1030
www.tcmpub.com

ISBN 978-1-4258-5895-7

© 2019 Teacher Created Materials, Inc.
Printed in Malaysia
Thumbprints.21254

Table of Contents

Wagging and Working 4

Assistance Dogs 6

Other Working Dogs 16

Canine Heroes 26

Problem Solving 28

Glossary 30

Index 31

Answer Key 32

Wagging and Working

What comes to mind when you think of dogs? You might imagine their playful barks, slobbery kisses, and boundless energy for games of fetch. However, certain dogs are more than just furry, lovable friends. They are specially trained, hardworking animals with important jobs—more than just getting the newspaper from the driveway!

Assistance dogs help people do things that they cannot easily do on their own. They can perform many different tasks, depending on what people need. Assistance dogs guide people who cannot see well. They bark when they hear noises to alert people who cannot hear well. Assistance dogs also help people open doors and turn off lights.

Working dogs perform different types of jobs. They may work with volunteers or members of the military. They sometimes work at airports or at hospitals. These dogs are often in intense situations, and they keep people safe.

Although these **canines** may look like normal pets, they have been trained to help people in their times of need. They keep people active, healthy, happy, and safe, and they do it all while wagging their tails.

Assistance Dogs

Turning the pages of a book, picking up shoes from the floor, or crossing the street may be simple tasks you do every day. But for people with **impairments** or **disabilities**, these tasks can be difficult or even impossible. Assistance dogs help these people.

Some people are visually impaired. They may be blind or have trouble seeing. Guide dogs help these people get around safely by guiding them as they walk.

Hearing-impaired people may have trouble hearing sounds. Or they may hear no sound at all. Hearing dogs listen for sounds. Then, they lead their **handlers** to the sources.

There are wide-ranging disabilities other than visual and hearing impairments. Some people may have health issues that need monitoring, while other people may not be able to walk. Service dogs assist these people.

All assistance dogs—guide, hearing, and service—play important roles in their handlers' lives. Remember not to pet assistance dogs if you see them in public. Petting them distracts them from their work. Assistance dogs need to focus on helping their handlers with daily tasks so their handlers can gain a new sense of freedom and safety.

This Labrador retriever is geared up to work as a service dog.

A guide dog helps its handler on an escalator.

This Labrador retriever is training to be a hearing dog.

A service dog helps its handler with his wallet.

Guide Dogs

For visually impaired people, moving around—even in their own homes—can be difficult. Guide dogs help them navigate their way through houses, streets, restaurants, buildings, and more. These dogs wear harnesses with handles that their handlers hold onto. The handlers choose where they want to go, and guide dogs make sure they stay safe along the way. Guide dogs are trained to stop when they see curbs, steps, tree branches, or anything else that may injure their handlers.

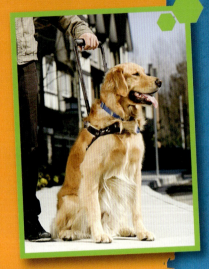

A guide dog helps its handler buy tickets for the subway.

Most guide dogs are large dogs, such as Labrador retrievers, golden retrievers, and German shepherds. Volunteers raise guide dog puppies for over a year, and then the dogs go to special schools. At school, they learn how to guide people. They also learn "intelligent disobedience." That means guide dogs will intentionally disobey their handlers to keep them from danger. For example, if a handler tells a guide dog to cross a street, but there is a car coming, the guide dog stays in place until it is safe. Once a guide dog can pass all its tests, the dog graduates and is matched with a handler.

This German shepherd works as a guide dog.

LET'S EXPLORE MATH

Guide dogs are trained for 4–6 months by professional trainers. Imagine that a professional organization tracks the number of months of training its dogs have completed so far. How can you use the bar graph to determine how many guide dogs it is training?

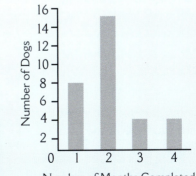

Guide Dog Training

Hearing Dogs

Hearing dogs assist people who are hearing impaired or deaf. Hearing dogs are trained to listen to sounds around them. They know how to filter those sounds and choose important, urgent ones that their handlers may want to know about, such as doorbells buzzing, babies crying, or telephones ringing. Hearing dogs are trained to touch their handlers to get their attention. They put their furry paws on their handlers' laps or nudge them with their wet noses. Then, they lead their handlers to the sources of the sounds.

Hearing dogs are usually small or medium **mixed-breed** dogs. Just like guide dogs, they go to special schools. At school, hearing dogs learn which sounds require responses. They learn the difference between safe sounds and danger sounds. For example, hearing dogs are trained to understand the difference between the sounds oven timers make and the sounds smoke detectors make. This way, hearing dogs know when they need to lead their handlers to the kitchen or quickly take them outside to safety.

LET'S EXPLORE MATH

People who need hearing dogs often request small- to medium-sized dogs. Breeds such as shelties, terriers, poodles, cockers, Lhasa apsos, shih tzus, and Chihuahuas are popular. Imagine that a training organization has 30 hearing dogs of different breeds. The staff tracks the dogs' weights in kilograms and records the data in a box plot.

1. What is the median weight of the hearing dogs? What does this number tell you?
2. How can you tell what the interquartile range of the data is?
3. Magda says that 15 dogs have weights between 5 and 7 kilograms. Is she correct? How do you know?

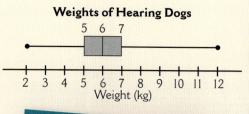

Weights of Hearing Dogs

This mixed-breed hearing dog rides with its handler to work.

A German shepherd mix listens for sounds.

This hearing dog "wakes up" its handler during a demonstration in London, England.

Service Dogs

Service dogs are the third type of assistance dog. Service dogs help people who have disabilities other than hearing or visual impairments. Service dogs help them with a wide range of tasks.

Most service dogs are either golden retrievers or Labrador retrievers. These dogs are medium sized, fun, and full of energy. These traits make them the perfect choice for helping people. There are two main types of service dogs: physical service dogs and **psychiatric** service dogs.

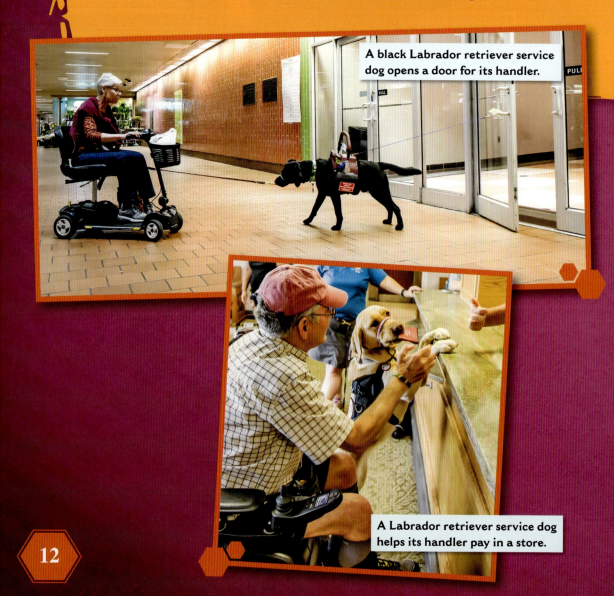

A black Labrador retriever service dog opens a door for its handler.

A Labrador retriever service dog helps its handler pay in a store.

Physical service dogs help people with physical tasks. They can open doors or turn off lights. They can help their handlers stand, or they can fetch things for their handlers. They can notify people that their handlers want to speak with them.

Physical service dogs can also help handlers monitor their health issues. For example, they can alert people with **diabetes** when their blood sugar levels are low. They can help people with **epilepsy** stay safe during **seizures**. Service dogs can also be trained to smell things in the air that their handlers are allergic to. They can alert their handlers to leave the area immediately to avoid allergic reactions.

An Australian shepherd service dog pushes a crosswalk button.

A handler instructs his service dog to push the automatic door button.

Psychiatric service dogs are specially trained to help people with **severe** mental disabilities. They help their handlers function in ways that they would not otherwise be able to do. For example, these dogs know how to distract their handlers if they sense a panic attack coming on. Or they can walk ahead of handlers with **post-traumatic stress disorder** (PTSD) to check that rooms are clear.

Both physical and psychiatric service dogs train for one to two years before they are given to handlers. They learn how to complete tasks that will help their handlers. They also learn how to behave and stay focused in public, which is a key part of their training. Service dogs have to be alert to small changes in their handlers' conditions. But they also have to be calm enough not to be removed from public places. Service dogs must know how to ignore distractions and to focus only on their handlers. At the end of their training, they must pass a series of tests. Then, they are **certified** as service dogs and given to handlers.

A PTSD psychiatric service dog naps while its handler eats lunch.

a psychiatric service dog and its handler

A service dog walks alongside its handler.

Other Working Dogs

There are many other canine helpers besides assistance dogs. Working dogs can be found almost anywhere. You may have even seen them before!

Therapy dogs visit people in many places, including hospitals, airports, and courtrooms. They calm people and improve their moods.

Military working dogs (MWDs) work for any branch of the **armed services**. These dogs spend their days in war zones with soldiers. Their jobs vary depending on where they are working or what their handlers need.

Screening dogs work at areas of mass transportation, such as train stations and airports. They might sniff people's luggage or be trained to smell dangerous chemicals. Screening dogs keep people safe when they travel.

Search and rescue dogs (SARs) work with volunteers to find missing people or people who are in danger. SARs work in different environments and are trained to track scents in all types of locations.

All working dogs perform very important tasks. They are highly trained, smart, and specialized in keeping people safe and calm.

A Labrador retriever screening dog sniffs luggage at an airport.

A German shepherd MWD works with the U.S. Army in Afghanistan.

A golden retriever SAR searches debris after an earthquake.

Therapy Dogs

A big hug, a hot bowl of soup, and a warm, fuzzy blanket can bring comfort to people who are feeling down. Therapy dogs have a similar effect—they bring comfort to people who need emotional support. These dogs visit people in hospitals or retirement homes and keep people happy and peaceful. They are sometimes found at airports, calming nervous travelers. Therapy dogs go to schools and help students feel better when they are anxious. Therapy dogs also visit college students who may feel sad being away from home for the first time. Therapy dogs are even used in courtrooms. They are trained to sit in **witness boxes** with children. These dogs help calm children who are in stressful situations.

A golden retriever therapy dog visits a girl in the hospital.

Before therapy dogs are allowed to visit people, they must pass 10 tests. These tests certify the dogs as "Canine Good Citizens." Once they pass those tests, they are allowed to work.

Therapy dogs come in all sizes and breeds. They have to be calm, patient, and love meeting new people. Unlike assistance dogs, which you shouldn't pet, therapy dogs love to be petted while they work!

LET'S EXPLORE MATH

Dr. Jack was the on-staff therapy dog at the Mayo Clinic in Minnesota. Before retiring, he visited patients every day. But many hospitals have therapy dogs that visit only on certain days. Imagine that volunteer handlers survey local hospitals. They ask how many days a week therapy dogs visit. They show their data in a dot plot.

1. Alwan and Laila are volunteer handlers. They work together to interpret the dot plot. Alwan says, "One hospital has 7 therapy dogs." Laila says, "One hospital has therapy dogs visit 7 days a week." How can you determine who is correct?

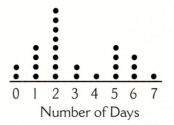

2. Use the dot plot to summarize the data.

   a. What does each dot on the dot plot represent?

   b. What are the mean and median of the data?

3. Draw a box plot to show the data. What is the interquartile range of the data? What does this number tell you?

Military Working Dogs

MWDs work for countries' armed services. In the United States, there are MWDs in all branches: army, navy, air force, coast guard, and marines. They go into dangerous places, usually in war zones, and keep their handlers safe.

MWDs in the United States train for about four months before they go into the field. The training for MWDs is intense. Half the dogs that enter the program do not graduate. During training, they learn basic commands and how to guard areas. They also learn how to track certain smells that could be dangerous. A key job for MWDs is sniffing out either explosives or **narcotics**. MWDs have such precise noses that they can smell these chemicals long before machines can. MWDs notify their handlers when they have found something and quickly lead handlers to the source of the scent.

MWDs retire when their health starts to worsen or if they are injured while working. More than 90 percent of MWD handlers adopt their dogs when the canines retire. The rest can be adopted by other people, or the dogs can undergo new training to work as police dogs (K9s) or as screening dogs.

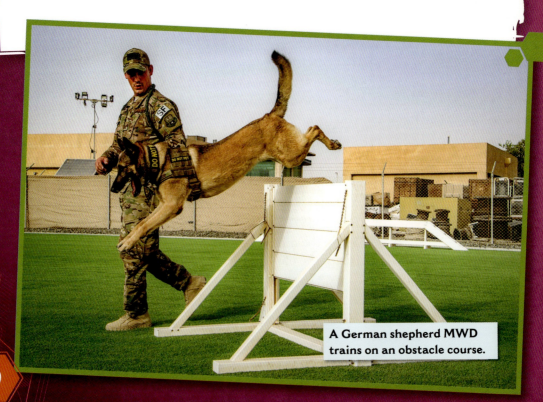

A German shepherd MWD trains on an obstacle course.

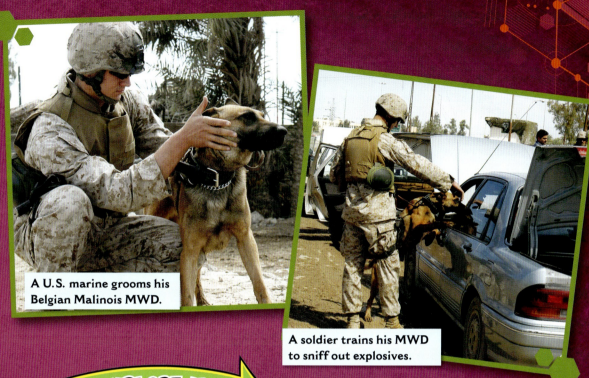

A U.S. marine grooms his Belgian Malinois MWD.

A soldier trains his MWD to sniff out explosives.

LET'S EXPLORE MATH

Veterinarians check MWDs to make sure they are fit, healthy, and able to work. Vets decide whether MWDs should retire based on health, not age. Some MWDs work up to 15 years! Imagine that a group of vets tracks how long the MWDs under their care have worked. They show the data in a histogram.

1. What data do the vets collect? What units of measurement do they use?

2. A vet says that he can't calculate the mean using the histogram, but he can estimate the median.

   a. Why can't he calculate the mean?

   b. What is the estimated median of the data?

   c. Why can he only estimate the median as opposed to finding an exact median?

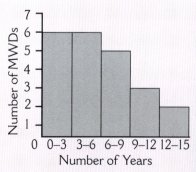

Number of Years that MWDs Have Worked

Screening Dogs

You may have seen screening dogs at airports, train stations, or ferry terminals. These efficient dogs keep hundreds of thousands of travelers safe each day. They check people and luggage in transportation centers for dangerous or illegal items.

Screening dogs and MWDs go through much of the same scent training. Screening dogs have 12 weeks of training before they can work. They learn how to deal with the sounds, smells, sights, and interruptions of busy public places. Screening dogs spend most of their workdays sniffing people. During training, they learn which scents can be dangerous. These dogs search for anything that could be unsafe or illegal. When they sniff out a dangerous scent, they quietly notify their handlers. Then, the handlers can search people or luggage to find the source of the scent.

When the dogs clear travelers, those people can go through security more quickly. This helps keep lines short at transportation centers. For example, airports that don't have screening dogs can check about 150 people per hour. With screening dogs, that number jumps to 250 people per hour!

A screening dog smells luggage at an airport in Missouri.

LET'S EXPLORE MATH

Currently, the U.S. Transportation Security Administration has over 900 passenger screening canine teams. The dogs and their handlers work to keep travelers safe and decrease wait times at security checkpoints. Imagine that checkpoint officers at different airports track passenger wait times in lines with and without screening dogs. They show the data in a table and a box plot.

1. Draw a box plot to show the data in the table. Use the same scale as the box plot below.

2. Imagine that a reporter is writing an article about passenger wait times. She wants to check her claims before posting them. Use your box plots to determine whether the claims are true or false. Justify your reasoning.

    a. The median passenger wait time is decreased by over 20 minutes in lines with screening dogs.

    b. The longest wait time in lines with screening dogs is less than the shortest wait time in lines without screening dogs.

    c. There is less variance in wait times in lines with screening dogs than without screening dogs.

Lines with Screening Dogs

Airport	Wait Time (minutes)
A	30
B	12
C	20
D	10
E	5
F	5
G	12
H	25
I	22
J	15
K	20
L	15

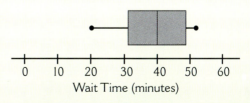

Lines without Screening Dogs

Wait Time (minutes)

Search and Rescue Dogs

Just like MWDs and screening dogs, SARs use their powerful senses of smell to help people. These brave dogs work with volunteers to find missing people or pets. They find people after **natural disasters**, building collapses, or other tragedies.

SAR dogs are trained in obedience, **agility**, and other specific skills. Some SARs are trained to be air-scenting dogs. These dogs help their handlers search for people, such as in the aftermath of earthquakes.

A SAR dog trains its air-scenting skills.

A German shepherd SAR dog trains in the snow in Bulgaria.

Other SARs are trained as trailing dogs. These dogs sniff clothing or objects from specific people, often missing people, and then pick up their scents. They can find people from about 1 mile (1.6 kilometers) away. Trailing SARs have an incredibly accurate sense of smell. A trailing SAR can tell where the person it is tracking turned and even where the person may have **backtracked**!

Successful SARs have a lot of energy and can stay engaged in a task for hours at a time. However, this single-minded focus can also be a danger to the dogs. Many SARs don't know how to pace themselves when working. Thanks to their strong bonds, handlers know when to give SARs a well-deserved break.

LET'S EXPLORE MATH

Many SAR teams are made up of highly trained volunteers. Dogs and their handlers train for about two years and have to pass tests before they are ready for missions. Volunteer SAR teams are on call 24 hours a day, 7 days a week if law enforcement requests their help. Imagine that a volunteer SAR organization tracks how many missions their teams complete each year. They show the data in a stem-and-leaf plot.

1. How can you determine how many years the organization has tracked its number of missions?

2. Do you think mean or median is the most appropriate measure of center for the data? Why?

Number of Missions Each Year

stem	leaf
0	1 8 8
1	1 1 3 3 4 4 5 7 7 7
2	3 4 6 6 6 8 8
3	3 5 7 8
4	2
5	2

Key:
2|3 means 23

Canine Heroes

Every day, people rely on working dogs' intelligence, bravery, and loyalty to their jobs. Assistance dogs perform tasks that their handlers cannot do themselves. Other working dogs keep people safe and make them feel better during times of stress. Dogs even find missing people and save lives!

Dog trainers and handlers test the limits of what these incredible canines can do. And dogs continue to go above and beyond what is asked of them. The future of what tasks dogs will do next is still to be explored. Anyone who is willing to work hard and have a lot of patience can train the next canine hero.

A New York police officer pets his German shepherd K9 partner.

However, the truth is, a dog does not have to guide blind people or sniff out dangerous scents to be a hero. All dogs can be heroes, whether they're playing fetch in the backyard or saving people from a collapsed building. Every dog has the ability to perform a priceless service each and every day—loving you. For a lot of people, that is the best kind of service a dog can perform!

Problem Solving

Before professional instructors train guide dogs, volunteers raise the puppies. College students are offering to be those volunteers! More than 18 colleges have clubs that allow students to raise the puppies right on campus. But it's not all fun and games. There's a lot of work involved too. Volunteers provide safe homes, healthy food, medical care, and toys. They teach the puppies manners and basic commands, such as *sit*, *down*, *come*, *rest*, and *forward*. They guide the puppies to walk on the left side of handlers. They **socialize** the puppies by taking them out in public. Volunteers must attend training classes and take the puppies to obedience classes. Also, they submit reports tracking their progress.

Imagine that Wanika, Timothy, and Rosana are members of the puppy-raising club at their college. For two weeks, they track the time they spend training their puppies. Their data is in the table on page 29. Use it to help them prepare for their next meeting.

1. Wanika is concerned that Timothy is not spending enough time training his puppy. She wants to make sure she understands the data before speaking with him about it. Create stem-and-leaf plots, box plots, or histograms to compare the training times of the volunteers. How can Wanika use the data displays to explain her concerns to Timothy?

2. Rosana is designing a flyer to encourage more students to join the puppy-raising club. She wants the flyer to be eye-catching, but also realistic, so students understand how much time is needed to train puppies. Design a flyer she can hang around campus. Use your data displays to make a claim about the typical amount of time necessary to train puppies. Include it on the flyer with other information and graphics that will get students interested in the club.

Puppy Training			
Day	Times (minutes)		
	Wanika	Timothy	Rosana
1	110	30	92
2	50	60	90
3	58	15	74
4	62	0	90
5	57	15	90
6	48	10	86
7	96	0	0
8	0	10	75
9	124	75	90
10	54	15	90
11	60	0	90
12	64	30	75
13	30	30	84
14	110	30	0

Glossary

agility—the ability to move easily and quickly

armed services—the military organizations, such as the navy, air force, and army, of a specific country

backtracked—turned around and went back over a course

canines—dogs

certified—approved as having met the official requirements needed to do particular work

diabetes—a disease in which a person's body can't properly control the amount of sugar in their blood

disabilities—conditions that limit or damage people's mental or physical abilities

epilepsy—a disorder where people can suddenly lose consciousness and have seizures

handlers—people who control or train animals

impairments—conditions in which part of people's minds or bodies are damaged

mixed-breed—domesticated animals that are mixtures of two or more breeds, or types, of the same species

narcotics—drugs that are usually dangerous and illegal

natural disasters—sudden, horrible events in nature, such as floods or tornadoes, that can result in serious damage

post-traumatic stress disorder—a mental condition that can affect someone who has had a difficult experience

psychiatric—relating to a branch of medicine that focuses on emotional or mental disorders

seizures—attacks in which people lose consciousness and have uncontrolled, violent movements of their bodies

severe—very serious

socialize—teach people or animals to behave in ways that are acceptable in society

witness boxes—areas in courtrooms where people sit or stand to talk about what they know or have seen

Index

assistance dogs, 4, 6, 12, 16, 19, 26

breeds, 10–11, 19

Dr. Jack, 19

German shepherds, 9, 11, 17, 20, 24, 26

golden retrievers, 9, 12, 17–18

guide dogs, 6–10

hearing dogs, 6–7, 10–11

Labrador retrievers, 6–7, 9, 12, 16

Mayo Clinic, 19

military working dogs (MWDs), 16–17, 20–22, 24

Minnesota, 19

physical service dogs, 12–14

police dogs (K9s), 20, 26

psychiatric service dogs, 12, 14–15

screening dogs, 16, 20, 22–24

search and rescue dogs (SARs), 16–17, 24–25

service dogs, 6–7, 12–15

therapy dogs, 16, 18–19

trainers, 9, 26

U.S. Transportation Security Administration, 23

volunteers, 4, 9, 16, 19, 24–25

Answer Key

Let's Explore Math

page 9
31 guide dogs; 8 + 15 + 4 + 4 = 31

page 10
1. 6 kg; Half the dogs weigh 6 kg or less, and half the dogs weigh 6 kg or more.
2. 2 kg; 7 − 5 = 2; The weights of the middle 50% of the dogs vary by 2 kg.
3. yes; There are 30 dogs, the weights of the middle 50% of the dogs are between 5 and 7 kg, and 50% of 30 is 15.

page 19
1. Laila; The dot plot shows how many days a week therapy dogs visit, not the number of therapy dogs.
2. a. one hospital that reported data
   b. mean: 3; median: 2
3. 3.5; 5 − 1.5 = 3.5; The number of days that therapy dogs visit the middle 50% of hospitals varies by 3.5 days.

Therapy Dog Visits
Number of Days

page 21
1. how long MWDs have worked; years
2. a. The vet can't calculate the mean without knowing individual data points.
   b. 3–6 years
   c. He can't find the exact median, but he can find out which interval contains the middle data point.

page 23
1.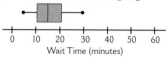
Lines without Screening Dogs
Wait Time (minutes)

2. a. true; 40 − 15 = 25 min.
   b. false; 30 min. is more than 20 min.
   c. true; With screening dogs, the variance is 25 min. (30 − 5), and without screening dogs, the variance is 32 min. (52 − 20).

page 25
1. 27 years; by counting the number of "leaves," or data points
2. Answers will vary. Example: *Median because the two high values impact the mean more than the median.*

Problem Solving
1. Answers will vary. Example: *More than 75% of Timothy's training times fall within the first quartile of Wanika and Rosana's training times.*

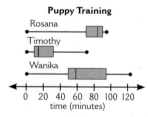
Puppy Training
Rosana
Timothy
Wanika
time (minutes)

2. Flyers should include a claim, graphics, and information. Example: *It is typical for students to spend about an hour or more every day training their puppy.*